Rev...

101 Things To Do...

Pull yourse...
plenty mo...

Nick Ferris

SUMMERSDALE

Copyright © Summersdale Publishers Ltd 2001

All rights reserved

No part of this book may be reproduced by any means, nor transmitted, nor translated into a machine language without the written permission of the publisher

Summersdale Publishers Ltd
46 West Street
Chichester
PO19 1RP   UK

www.summersdale.com

ISBN 1 84024 192 6

Printed and bound in Great Britain

Text by Nick Ferris
Additional material by Simon Clews
Cartoons by Kate Taylor

What did the cannibal do after
he dumped his girlfriend?

He wiped his arse.

Introduction

Revenge offers an amusing guide to the opportunities open to the person who suddenly finds themselves single again and is quite frankly pissed off about it.

How do you get back at the person who dumped you?

Well, look no further. There are many different ways. Some are funny. Some are silly. Many are disgusting. Some are dangerous. Some are unthinkable. This book has them all. Plus a few more.

Dumping happens to us all. The Royals, the Pope, presidents, rock stars, dentists, funeral directors, road sweepers, bankers, jockeys, even Wombles and Teletubbies get dumped. This book is for all of you and those in-between.

Revenge takes no responsibility for any actions whatsoever of anyone dead, alive, human, alien or just plain dumb.

REVENGE!

Get your partner into a drunken stupor and cut their hair off...

Which body part you shave depends on the severity of your feelings:

Suicidal: All body hair
Depressed: Groin and legs
Damaged ego: Eyebrows

101 THINGS TO DO WHEN YOU'VE BEEN DUMPED

REVENGE!

Invent a time machine...

Go back and dump your ex ten minutes before they dumped you.

Please note - Instructions to build a time machine have not been included with this pocket guide due to time constraints.

101 THINGS TO DO WHEN YOU'VE BEEN DUMPED

REVENGE!

Cook a wholesome homemade pie... with dog food...

Whether or not you tell them is up to you. If they are prone to projectile vomiting, have a bucket ready when you tell them face to face. Then run.

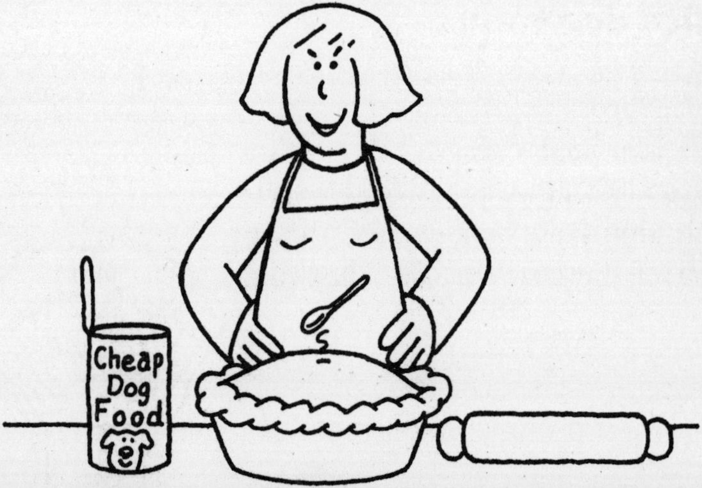
Cheap
Dog
Food

REVENGE!

Just say...

"It was love at first sight, but then I took another look"

101 THINGS TO DO WHEN YOU'VE BEEN DUMPED

Phone up the Australian speaking clock...

Sneak into your ex's house and call the Australian speaking clock when they're at work, leaving it off the hook. Sex lines in Columbia work just as well. But your ex may like that though.

REVENGE!

Put your ex's name down for a music club so they end up buying overpriced CDs for the rest of their life...

If you're really clever, you can keep the five free CD's offered and they will have to buy Editor's Choice of country classics every month for a year.

101 THINGS TO DO WHEN YOU'VE BEEN DUMPED

Do a Geri Halliwell...

Go on crash diet and then go out with much better looking people than your ex.

REVENGE!

While your ex is on holiday, turn them into a star...

Rig their house up with Big Brother-style webcams and broadcast their habits to the world on their return. But don't tell them!

101 THINGS TO DO WHEN YOU'VE BEEN DUMPED

Leave a note on your ex's doorstep for the milkman...

Declare their undying love for him and ask him out for a date.

REVENGE!

Train your ex's Goldfish to go on hunger strike in sympathy...

Make some little signs like 'We want YOUR NAME back'

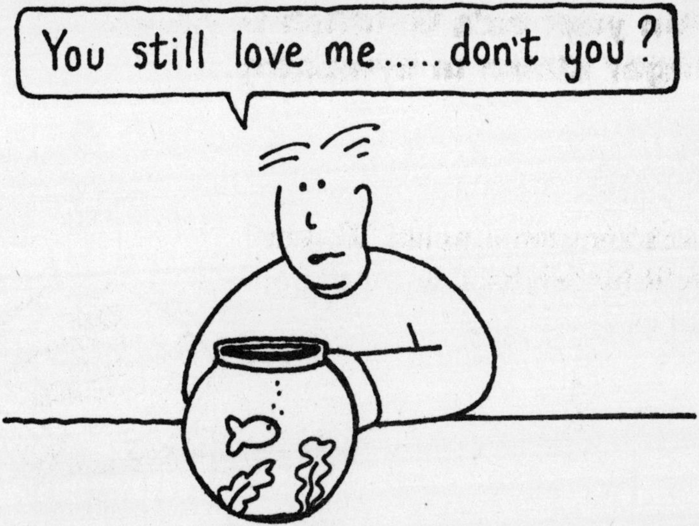
You still love me..... don't you?

REVENGE!

Hold a party...

Invite everyone you know and everyone your ex knows. Apart from your ex.

20

101 THINGS TO DO WHEN YOU'VE BEEN DUMPED

Cook crispy fried worms as part of a farewell dinner...

Nice with mayonnaise.

REVENGE!

Use the gift of tattoo...

Get your ex inebriated beyond belief and take them to tattoo parlour.

Suggestions - For Sale / Sold / I'm Gay / Kick Me

101 THINGS TO DO WHEN YOU'VE BEEN DUMPED

REVENGE!

Say it with pizza...

Call your local pizza parlour, tell them you are having a party and order 40 pizzas with extra toppings they hate. Works even better if they don't like pizza.

101 THINGS TO DO WHEN YOU'VE BEEN DUMPED

REVENGE!

Spend your ex's money on mail order catalogues — irons, cheap bedspreads or mobile phone deckchairs...

Only buy things you know they hate, don't need, can't afford and / or don't fit. Anything that hits all four revenge categories is perfect.

101 THINGS TO DO WHEN YOU'VE BEEN DUMPED

"I'd like to order everything, twice over."

Useless tat Catalogue

REVENGE!

Hire a Hypnotist...

To hypnotise your ex and make them make beg for forgiveness to have you back. Good opportunity to get rid of all those bad habits too.

101 THINGS TO DO WHEN YOU'VE BEEN DUMPED

Hire an expensive car for the day...

Visit your ex and say 'Look darling, this is what I bought for your birthday. Never mind.' And drive off. If they can't drive, put some L-plates on.

REVENGE!

Go out with one of your ex's parents...

So you can execute parental power over them – the ultimate revenge. Make them go to bed at 7pm, that kind of thing.

101 THINGS TO DO WHEN YOU'VE BEEN DUMPED

REVENGE!

Send an embarrassing note to your ex's parents...

Whilst complimenting them on their choice of tie-back frilly curtains, casually drop in lines such as:

'Your son/daughter's constant desire to wear a bin liner and say 'look at me, I'm a black hole' made me realise we just weren't made for each other...'

Revenge warning: A similar letter could be sent to your parents. Can you get up early enough to check the post every day?

101 THINGS TO DO WHEN YOU'VE BEEN DUMPED

Invoice your ex for all the time you've spent together...

Charge double time for all the physchological trauma you had to listen to, from whether their bum looked big to his constant questioning of whether he was any good in bed. This is not tax deductible though.

REVENGE!

Say it with flowers...

Send bunch of dead, smelling flowers to where they work with a card saying they reminded you of him/her.

101 THINGS TO DO WHEN YOU'VE BEEN DUMPED

Just say...

"I've never been able to get you out of my head, but I'm saving up for a lobotomy."

REVENGE!

Clone your ex...

Take a blood sample whilst they are not looking, buy a junior chemist kit and some books on cloning from your local library. Once complete either continue the relationship or just dump them first.

101 THINGS TO DO WHEN YOU'VE BEEN DUMPED

REVENGE!

Write a resignation letter to your ex's boss...

If part of you is now unemployed, why shouldn't they be?

101 THINGS TO DO WHEN YOU'VE BEEN DUMPED

Suggest 'one last time'...

Get your partner naked and then take a picture, saying 'another one for the collection. That's eighty-four now'.

REVENGE!

Hire a plane to fly a banner in the sky saying 'Gary/Tracey's crap in bed'...

Avoid cloudy days otherwise the impact is pretty negligible.

101 THINGS TO DO WHEN YOU'VE BEEN DUMPED

REVENGE!

Spend £10,000 on plastic surgery...

So your ex no longer recognises you. This way you get to go out with them again and dump them next time round should you desire.

101 THINGS TO DO WHEN YOU'VE BEEN DUMPED

Phone the child support agency...

If you're female and you've just been dumped, why not phone the child support agency and pretend that he's left you holding the baby. Borrow a baby if necessary and spend your new nappy allowance on cocktail chasers.

REVENGE!

Go out with your ex's younger sister / brother...

Saves having to learn a new surname too…

101 THINGS TO DO WHEN YOU'VE BEEN DUMPED

Become a world famous rock star...

Guaranteed to piss off your ex. Make sure you mention their name in interviews and rub in how much fun you are having without them holding you back.

REVENGE!

Book a haircut for your ex...

Get 30 hairdressers to call on your ex for a home visit simultaneously. Get a dog cutter while you're at it too.

Works much better if your ex is bald and has no sense of humour.

101 THINGS TO DO WHEN YOU'VE BEEN DUMPED

Just say...

"Well actually I think we should have finished ages ago but I didn't have the heart to tell you."

Go upstairs, scribble a dumping note and produce as evidence that you were going to give it to them. Back-date it.

REVENGE!

Cut ex's bra in half to be really annoying...

If you worship bras too much to be so cruel, try laddering all her tights.

101 THINGS TO DO WHEN YOU'VE BEEN DUMPED

Put hair remover in their shampoo...

If that's too extreme, how about bright pink hair dye?

REVENGE!

Profit from their loss...

Refuse to give back your ex's belongings and put them up for sale on an online auction (see www.eBay.com etc).

Use the money to get very drunk or send to a worthy cause such as a Dyslexic Donkey Retreat.

101 THINGS TO DO WHEN YOU'VE BEEN DUMPED

If your ex is religious...

Send a note to their local church asking for their views on sex with animals. Say you are finding the temptation hard to deal with and can't find anything in the Bible that says it is bad.

REVENGE!

Become a witch...

Don't put a curse on your ex that you may regret, such as a two-headed pig. You may change your mind and want them back for more than just breakfast. Ability to hackle and a broom a distinct advantage.

101 THINGS TO DO WHEN YOU'VE BEEN DUMPED

Disguise yourself as a fortune-teller...

Read your ex's palm, telling them that dumping you showed the worst lack of judgement since Hear'Say got their contract.

REVENGE!

Go public...

Go on a Jerry Springer type show, and invite your ex. Then hire 50 people to appear and claim to be your lover and fight over you.

101 THINGS TO DO WHEN YOU'VE BEEN DUMPED

Just say...

'I was only joking when I said "No, you're not fat"'

REVENGE!

Pour grass seed on carpet...

This can only be effectively done if ex-partner is away for at least a week. To be really cruel break the lawnmower too.

101 THINGS TO DO WHEN YOU'VE BEEN DUMPED

Go for their green-fingered heart...

If your ex loves their lawn, salt is an excellent way of killing the grass. Alternatively, cover the lawn with bread late at night and they'll be woken by a bird garden party, with a few guest ants no doubt.

REVENGE!

The old dog poo fire trick...

Find some dog poo (available from any dog's bottom) and place in a bag. Then take round to your ex and just before you ring the doorbell, set the bag on fire.

Your ex will see the flames and stamp on the bag to put them out.

101 THINGS TO DO WHEN YOU'VE BEEN DUMPED

Apply for hundreds of jobs...

Under your ex's name, giving their current employer as full reference. Make them menial jobs like litter collector or white line painter too.

Don't Get Mad. GET REVENGE

REVENGE!

Blind Date...

Get one of your friends to call up your ex, say they saw him/her and would like to meet for a hot date. Make sure your friend doesn't turn up and have a hot date otherwise this revenge will backfire somewhat.

101 THINGS TO DO WHEN YOU'VE BEEN DUMPED

Just say...

"I only went out with you because your friends paid me."

(Produce a bundle of notes or receipts to add to the tale).

REVENGE!

Send a letter to HM Customs in your ex's name...

Ask for a permit to import class A drugs. Mention that they are fed up having to go to dealers.

101 THINGS TO DO WHEN YOU'VE BEEN DUMPED

Text Message revenge...

Send a note to a new lover saying how great you feel and free and send it to your ex by mistake, but on purpose.

REVENGE!

Invite some squatters into your ex's house...

Make sure they feel at home and know where the drinks cabinet is kept.

101 THINGS TO DO WHEN YOU'VE BEEN DUMPED

Say you only went out with them for their money...

Don't say this if your ex is broke. If they are very poor say you only went out with them as a social experiment. (produce some kind of official government badge at this juncture to reinforce the message. Failing that, a Tesco's Clubcard flashed quickly may fool them.)

REVENGE!

Revenge in Ignorance...

When your ex announces they have dumped you just say 'Pardon' and stick your finger in your ear. If you can't hear them, they can't dump you.

If your ex starts to write it down instead, simply act out sudden blindness.

101 THINGS TO DO WHEN YOU'VE BEEN DUMPED

REVENGE!

Go out with Pamela Anderson / Tom Cruise...

Be adventurous, date both to really annoy your ex.

101 THINGS TO DO WHEN YOU'VE BEEN DUMPED

Wake up call...

Arrange for the phone company to give your ex a 3 am wake up call every day for a year.

REVENGE!

Wait until your ex remarries...

And then turn up with a pillow under your dress, or hire a small child for the day if it's been more than nine months since you split up. Just shout 'what about the baby?!' at an inconvenient moment for perfect revenge.

101 THINGS TO DO WHEN YOU'VE BEEN DUMPED

Faxing Hell...

Glue two pieces to paper together, and fax your ex's machine in a continuous loop. Maybe draw a picture of a happy face with your name underneath if you don't mind detection.

REVENGE!

Not the car!...

If your ex has a white car, why not turn it into a Dalmatian with a tin of spray paint and cardboard with circle cut out? If you're feeling particularly vengeful go straight for the paint stripper.

101 THINGS TO DO WHEN YOU'VE BEEN DUMPED

Cement in the letter box...

Good way to stop them writing to any new lovers for a while, at least.

REVENGE!

Wet the bed...

Pour water on the sheets and cover them over. If you're feeling brave, why not add some texture too? A jelly, some sponge, a chocolate whip, all nicely mixed together.

101 THINGS TO DO WHEN YOU'VE BEEN DUMPED

Send letter to ex's landlord...

Giving notice, telling them how much they smell and how you can't wait to get out of that shit hole.

REVENGE!

Bumper Sticker their car...

'my bum is actually bigger than this bumper'

'yes my penis is really that small'

101 THINGS TO DO WHEN YOU'VE BEEN DUMPED

Insects through the letterbox...

Such as crickets will cause nice irritation for your ex.

REVENGE!

Use this checklist to see how corny they are when they dump you...

The more phrases they use, the better you'll feel about being dumped by someone so predictable. Send them a copy to get your revenge.

101 THINGS TO DO WHEN YOU'VE BEEN DUMPED

It's me, not you

I feel trapped

The spark has died

I think we should just be friends

I'm just not ready to commit myself

It just doesn't feel right anymore

I can't see a future with you

I just don't love you anymore

I'm in love with Michael Barrymore

REVENGE!

Cancel all of your ex's credit cards...

Works even better if you persuade them to take you out to dinner as a final gesture and then you quietly escape via the toilet before the bill arrives.

101 THINGS TO DO WHEN YOU'VE BEEN DUMPED

Put your ex's picture online...

See www.urdumped.co.uk - full of great dumping and revenge stories. See also www.cyberdumped.com

REVENGE!

Leave a note on their windscreen for all to see...

'Will be back soon. Gone off to masturbate.' For him.

'Back soon. Just ripping someone else's heart out.' For him or her.

101 THINGS TO DO WHEN YOU'VE BEEN DUMPED

Arrange a lobotomy for your ex...

So they forget they ever dumped you. Similar to time machine, but cheaper.

REVENGE!

Become an idiot...

Your ex will never have the satisfaction of dumping you because you can just sit on their garden fence and giggle inanely as though life is perfect.

101 THINGS TO DO WHEN YOU'VE BEEN DUMPED

Have a sex change...

Become your ex's partner's gay lover and then dump them. They'll be gutted and also very confused about their sexual orientation.

REVENGE!

Laughter...

Laugh maniacally when they dump you.

101 THINGS TO DO WHEN YOU'VE BEEN DUMPED

REVENGE!

Go out on a date within minutes.

And makes sure your ex sees you living life to the full and being ecstatically happy.

101 THINGS TO DO WHEN YOU'VE BEEN DUMPED

REVENGE!

Just say...

'I only went out with you as part of a bet anyway... hardly worth it for a fiver.'

101 THINGS TO DO WHEN YOU'VE BEEN DUMPED

Post your ex's number on a beastiality forum...

If that's too cruel, put them down as an expert on 18th Century Dolls and offer a free 24 hour advice line.

REVENGE!

Order a truckload of rocks to be dumped on your ex's garden...

Now you've both been dumped on.

101 THINGS TO DO WHEN YOU'VE BEEN DUMPED

Say you faked every orgasm (not recommended for men to say)...

There is nothing more damaging to the male ego than to think that the person you thought you were giving heavenly pleasure to was lying there counting the spiders on the ceiling.

REVENGE!

Win the National Lottery...

And give money to everyone apart from your ex. The odds are 1 in 13,983,816 to win whereas the odds for being struck by lightning are 1 in 709,260. It therefore may be easier to get revenge by inviting your ex to a field during the next thunderstorm.

101 THINGS TO DO WHEN YOU'VE BEEN DUMPED

Put an advert in the paper announcing what a bastard your ex is (see libel laws)...

Just a photo and caption will suffice: Warning! This person is an arsehole.

REVENGE!

Hire a Fortune Teller...

To go round your ex's house and give them the bleakest future imaginable unless they go back out with you.

I see no continuous stream of love-hungry, nubile, young babes.

REVENGE!

Just say...

"Well, I never could find your clitoris."

101 THINGS TO DO WHEN YOU'VE BEEN DUMPED

Hire a private detective...

To investigate the person you've been dumped for and send your ex a dossier so they'll have you back.

Don't Get Mad. GET REVENGE

REVENGE!

...eese in Car Heater...

Any cheese will do – will provide a smell like no other when your ex puts on the heater. Try also fish, eggs and maybe some unwashed socks for good measure.

101 THINGS TO DO WHEN YOU'VE BEEN DUMPED

Get a Dumpagram...

Get someone to dress up as Tarzan or Beelzebub to go to your ex's desk and sing a message about how crap they are generally.

101

REVENGE!

Pour sand in your ex's petrol tank...

For those people who love their cars more than you. Sand in the tank will bugger the engine and they won't be going anywhere.

If no sand available, just leave the headlights on all night. Remember to cancel their AA subscription first.

101 THINGS TO DO WHEN YOU'VE BEEN DUMPED

Order a subscription to Mayfair/ Lesbian Lust in ex's name...

Have it sent to workplace for added embarrassment.

REVENGE!

Beg for another go. When they say yes, simply dump them first this time.

Finish off by saying 'Don't look so upset, you'll find someone else, someday... try the blind hospice...'

101 THINGS TO DO WHEN YOU'VE BEEN DUMPED

Call the Samaritans...

Leave your ex's number, pretend to be suicidal and hang up. They'll call back and revenge will be sweet.

REVENGE!

Become a bus driver on your ex's bus route, and simply never let them on...

Just say, 'sorry, no ugly people on my bus' when they try to get on.

101 THINGS TO DO WHEN YOU'VE BEEN DUMPED

Make your ex a lovely dessert with extra lashings of laxatives...

If you do give this, make sure they leave pretty quickly otherwise you'll have to clear up the mess in the toilet, especially if they had the dog food pie for main course.

And turn off any gas appliances.

REVENGE!

Spice up their life...

Take their spice rack and mix up all the spices. Add some chilli into everything too.

101 THINGS TO DO WHEN YOU'VE BEEN DUMPED

Just say...

"I'll never forget the first time I met you, but I'll keep trying"

REVENGE!

Launch a website where everyone who ever went out with your ex can put up comments about how bad they were in bed ...

Send round the website address to all of your ex's colleagues too.

101 THINGS TO DO WHEN YOU'VE BEEN DUMPED

Sign your ex up for the army / French Foreign Legion...

You never know your luck, they may join and you'll be rid of them for at least a few years.

REVENGE!

Write to an agony aunt...

To publicise what your ex has done to you. Even better, call up a daytime chat programme and mention their name as many times as you can on air.

101 THINGS TO DO WHEN YOU'VE BEEN DUMPED

Go out with best friend...

Buy them far more flowers, take them to much nicer places and pick your nose less – guaranteed to wind up ex.

REVENGE!

Just say...

"Of course I said you were my first. I say that to everybody."

101 THINGS TO DO WHEN YOU'VE BEEN DUMPED

Write a number one song about your ex and how you are now over them...

Avoid phrases like 'I would die for you', 'nothing compares to you' and 'you are my everything' as this will only serve to boost your ex's ego.

REVENGE!

Take their favourite pet hostage...

Refuse to give back the pet until they apologise and realise the errors of their ways. Send some fur in the post just to scare them.

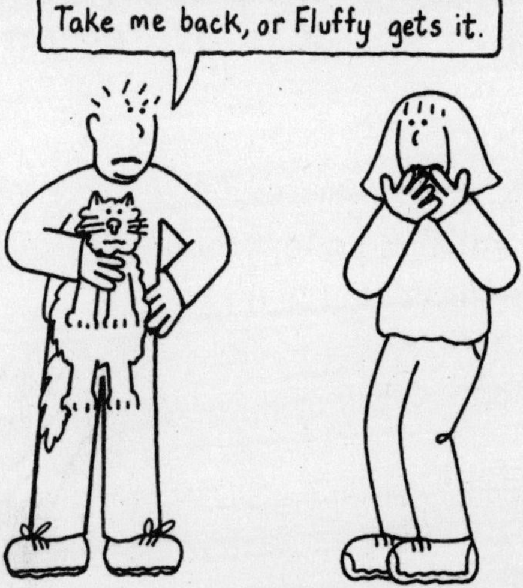
Take me back, or Fluffy gets it.

REVENGE!

Send anonymous emails to your ex complaining about poor body odour at work...

Lots of sites will send anonymous tips for you, such as

www.justatip.com or

www.thepayback.com

101 THINGS TO DO WHEN YOU'VE BEEN DUMPED

Walk around their local town with a megaphone and sign...

A great way of getting attention. Just hurl abuse about them, whilst carrying unflattering pictures of them eating a rancid pie.

REVENGE!

Dye ex's clothes pink...

Buy a cheap red T-shirt and simply bundle all their favourite clothes into the washing machine.

101 THINGS TO DO WHEN YOU'VE BEEN DUMPED

Do absolutely nothing...

This page is for jammy people
who never get dumped.

REVENGE!

And Finally... the sexist ones...

For Him...

Buy a dishwasher instead. That will show her.

101 THINGS TO DO WHEN YOU'VE BEEN DUMPED

For Her...

Buy some new batteries for the vibrator and get him where it hurts.

'I am free of all prejudice. I hate everyone equally.'

W C Fields

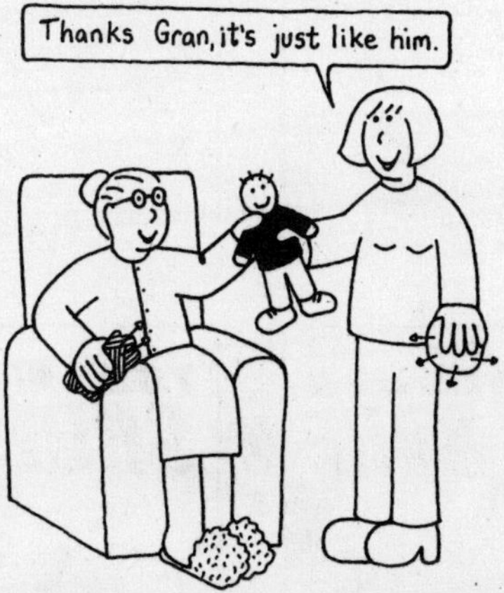
Thanks Gran, it's just like him.

EMMA BURGESS
YOU KNOW YOU'RE
GETTING OLD
WHEN...
I remember when all this was just a field.......
summersdale humour

EMMA BURGESS
YOU KNOW YOU'RE A
TELLY ADDICT
WHEN...
summersdale humour

MICHELLE LEGGATT
YOU KNOW YOU'RE A
SPORTS BORE
WHEN...
Not now love,
I'm off to get a round in.
summersdale humour

MICHELLE LEGGATT
YOU KNOW YOU'RE A
SHOPAHOLIC
WHEN...
BORN TO SHOP
summersdale humour

EMMA BURGESS
YOU KNOW YOUR
DIET ISN'T WORKING
WHEN...
FULL FAT FOOD
summersdale humour

EMMA BURGESS
YOU KNOW YOU'RE A
MANEATER
WHEN...
summersdale humour

EMMA BURGESS
YOU KNOW YOU'RE A
MOBILE ADDICT
WHEN...
summersdale humour

YOU KNOW YOU'RE A
COMPUTER NERD
WHEN...
SUMMERSDALE

For the latest humour books from Summersdale, check out

www.summersdale.com